What Would You Eat in the Rain Forest?

by Caroline Hutchinson

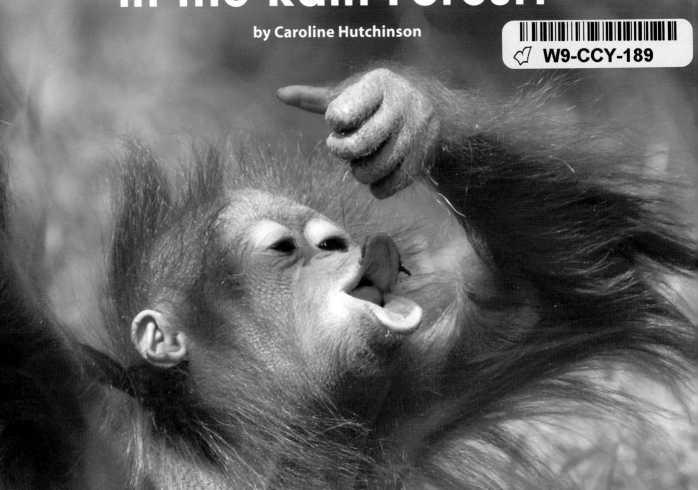

Many animals live in the rain forest.
Some animals eat fruit. Some eat
other animals.

The anteater has a very long nose.

It uses its nose to find ants.

The toucan has a very big beak.

It uses its beak to pick fruit to eat.

The monkey goes from
tree to tree.

Monkeys like fruit, but they
eat bugs, too.

The crocodile eats frogs.

When the crocodile sees a frog,
it swims very fast!

The jaguar climbs on a tree
to look for food.

Will it jump down to catch this crocodile?

The snake has very sharp teeth.

The snake uses its teeth
to catch mice.

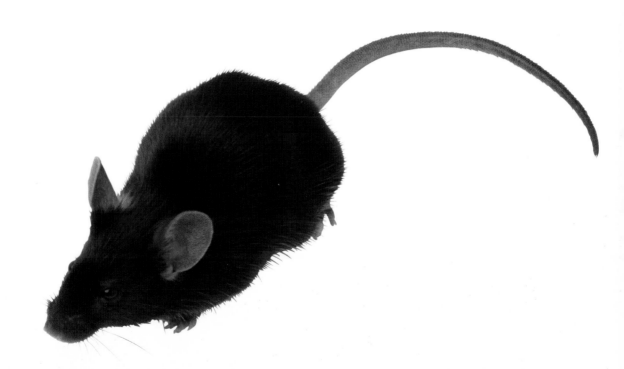

Would you eat a crocodile or mouse? Would you eat ants or fruit? What would you eat in the rain forest?